Copyright 2019 Gumdrop Press

All rights reserved.

ISBN-13: 978-1-945887-70-3

No part of this book may be reproduced in any written, electronic, or photocopied form without written permission of the publisher or author.

Every effort has been made to ensure the accuracy of the information contained in this book. The author and publisher disclaim liability to any party for any loss, damage, or disruption caused by errors or omissions that may result from the use of information contained within, whether such errors or omissions result from negligence, accident, or any other cause.

2020

Sun.	Mon.	Tue.	Wed.	Thu.	Fri.	Sat.
			1 New Year's Day	2	3	4
5	6	7	8	9	10	11
12	13	14	15	16	17	18
19	20 Martin Luther King, Jr. Day	21	22	23	24	25
26	27	28	29	30	31	

2020 February

Sun.	Mon.	Tue.	Wed.	Thu.	Fri.	Sat.
						1
2	3	4	5	6	7	8
9	10	11	12	13	14 Valentine's Day	15
16	17 Presidents' Day	18	19	20	21	22
23	24	25	26	27	28	29

2020

March

Sun.	Mon.	Tue.	Wed.	Thu.	Fri.	Sat.
1	2	3	4	5	6	7
8 **Daylight Saving Time Begins**	9	10	11	12	13	14
15	16	17 **St. Patrick's Day**	18	19	20	21
22	23	24	25	26	27	28
29	30	31				

2020

Sun.	Mon.	Tue.	Wed.	Thu.	Fri.	Sat.
					1	2
3	4	5	6	7	8	9
10 Mother's Day	11	12	13	14	15	16
17	18	19	20	21	22	23
24	25 Memorial Day	26	27	28	29	30
31						

2020 — June

Sun.	Mon.	Tue.	Wed.	Thu.	Fri.	Sat.
	1	2	3	4	5	6
7	8	9	10	11	12	13
14	15	16	17	18	19	20
21 Father's Day	22	23	24	25	26	27
28	29	30				

2020

July

Sun.	Mon.	Tue.	Wed.	Thu.	Fri.	Sat.
			1	2	3 Independence Day Observed	4 Independence Day
5	6	7	8	9	10	11
12	13	14	15	16	17	18
19	20	21	22	23	24	25
26	27	28	29	30	31	

2020

Sun.	Mon.	Tue.	Wed.	Thu.	Fri.	Sat.
						1
2	3	4	5	6	7	8
9	10	11	12	13	14	15
16	17	18	19	20	21	22
23	24	25	26	27	28	29
30	31					

2020

September

Sun.	Mon.	Tue.	Wed.	Thu.	Fri.	Sat.
		1	2	3	4	5
6	7 Labor Day	8	9	10	11	12
13	14	15	16	17	18	19
20	21	22	23	24	25	26
27	28	29	30			

2020

Sun.	Mon.	Tue.	Wed.	Thu.	Fri.	Sat.
				1	2	3
4	5	6	7	8	9	10
11	12 Columbus Day	13	14	15	16	17
18	19	20	21	22	23	24
25	26	27	28	29	30	31 Halloween

2020 — November

Sun.	Mon.	Tue.	Wed.	Thu.	Fri.	Sat.
1 Daylight Saving Time Ends	2	3 Election Day	4	5	6	7
8	9	10	11 Veterans Day	12	13	14
15	16	17	18	19	20	21
22	23	24	25	26 Thanksgiving Day	27	28
29	30					

2020

Sun.	Mon.	Tue.	Wed.	Thu.	Fri.	Sat.
		1	2	3	4	5
6	7	8	9	10	11	12
13	14	15	16	17	18	19
20	21	22	23	24	25 Christmas Day	26
27	28	29	30	31 New Year's Eve		